Tutti gli animali grandi e piccolo

Coloring Book

Young Scholar

All rights reserved. No part of this document may be reproduced
Used or transmitted in any form or by any means, electronic or otherwise. This means you
cannot photocopy any material ideas or tips that are provided in this book.

Young Scholar
An imprint of Ciparum LLC

Tutti gli animali grandi e piccoli Coloring Book
© 2017 Ciparum LLC
All rights reserved.
ISBN-10:1-63589-243-0
ISBN-13:978-1-63589-243-7

www.youngscholar.co

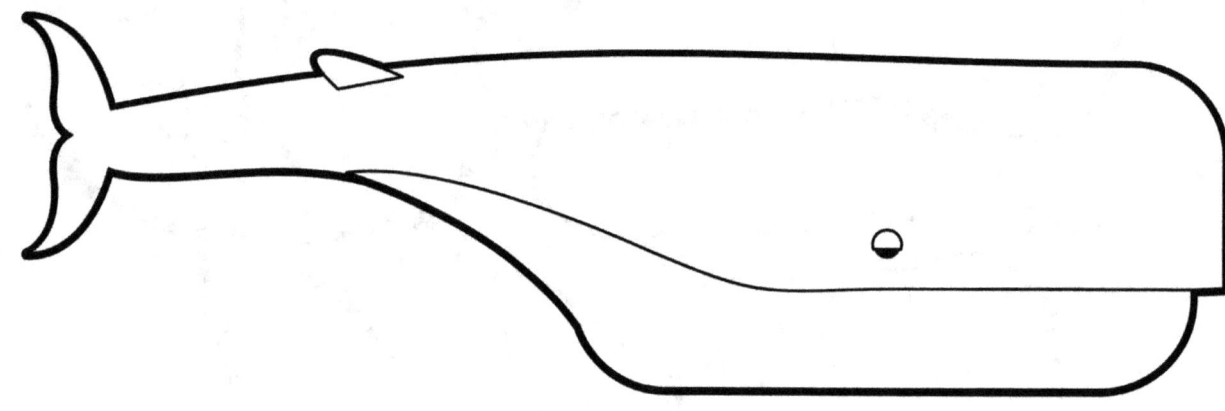

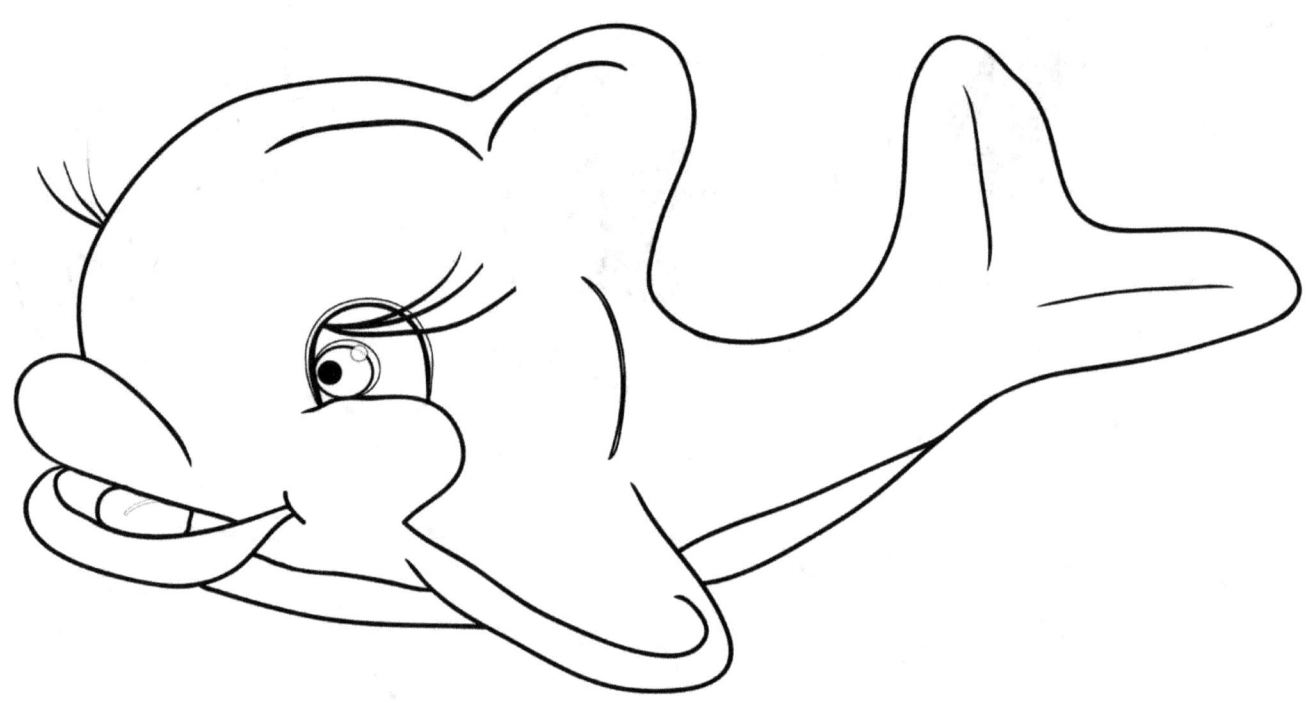

www.ingramcontent.com/pod-product-compliance
Lightning Source LLC
Chambersburg PA
CBHW051430070526
44584CB00023B/3663